MW00415387

To:

_____

Message:

_____

_____

_____

Love from:

_____

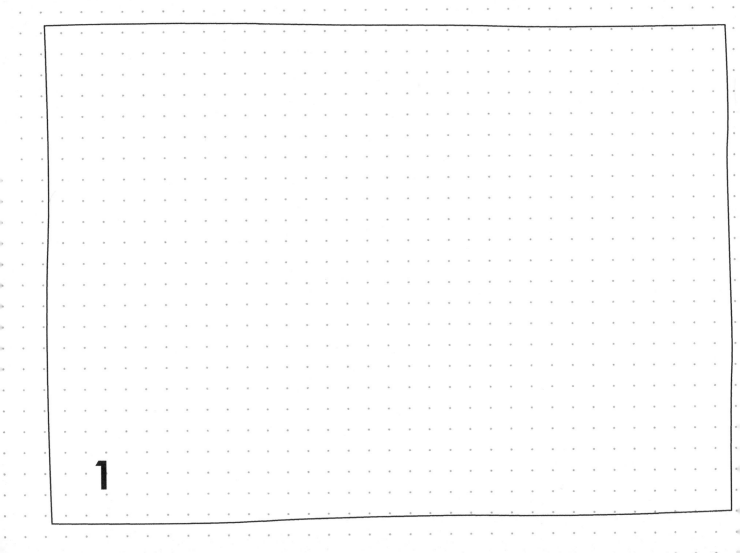

1

I love the way you

_____

in the morning.

2

I'm impressed by the way you

_____

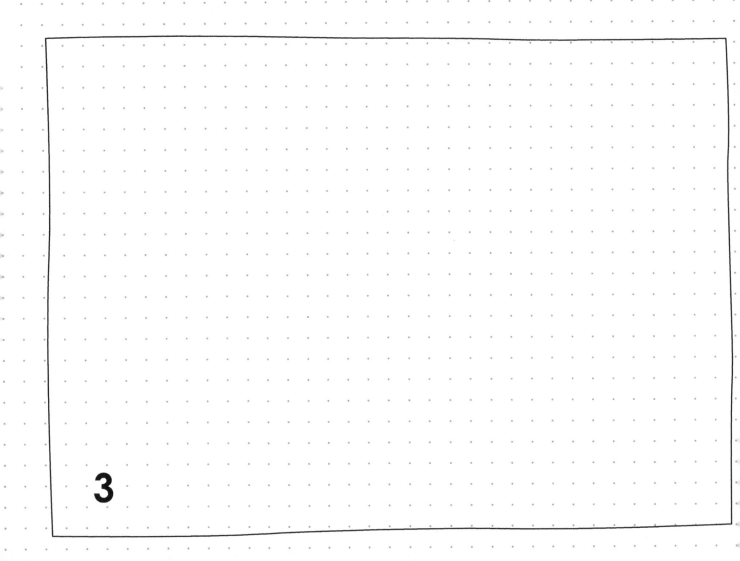

3

That funny thing you do with your

_____

whenever you're feeling

_____

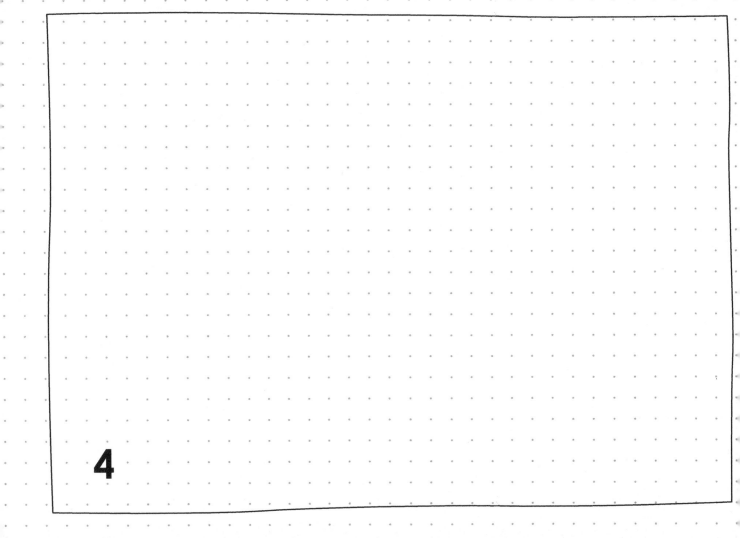

4

You are so

_____

with my friends and family.

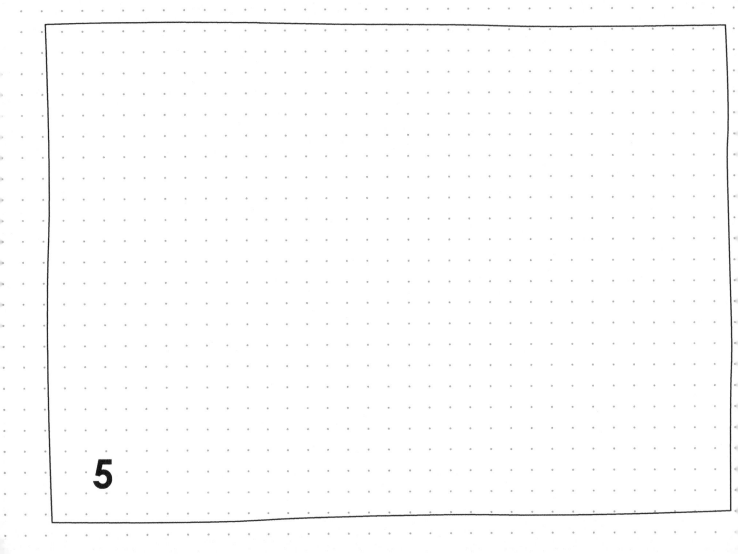

5

If it wasn't for you, I wouldn't

_____

6

The cute way you say

_____

7

I love how you need me to

_____

8

You do the goofiest things when

_____

9

That face you pull when you're

_____

makes me

_____

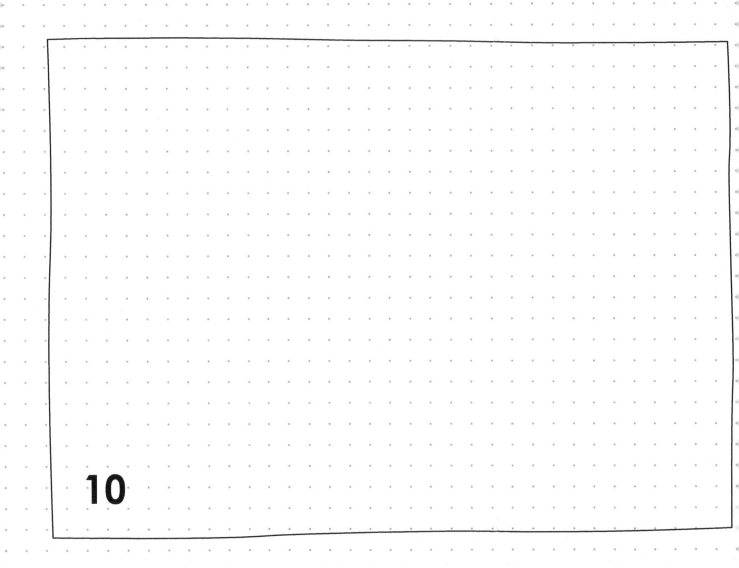

10

The way you

_____

when you get nervous.

11

You always make me

_____

whenever I want it.

12

You make every moment I spend with you

_____

13

I love how you

_____

when you're tired.

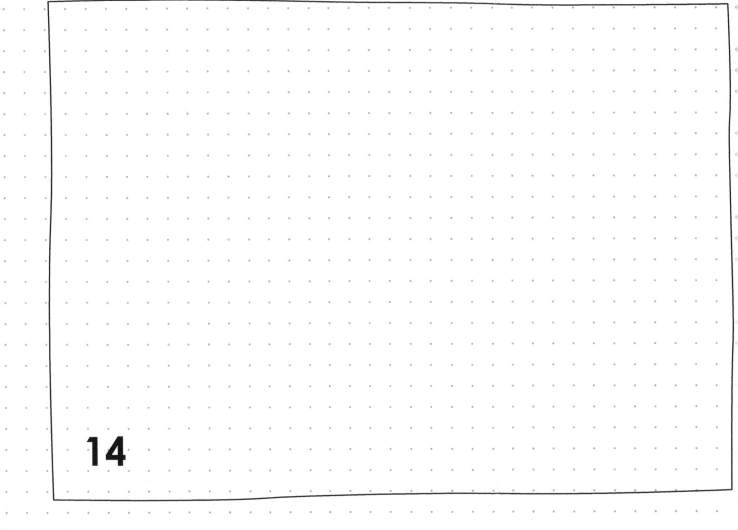

14

You have the most amazing

_____

15

I love sharing

_____

with you.

16

When you

_____

you take my breath away.

17

I love how you laugh when

_____

18

The way you take care of

_____

inspires me so much.

19

You have the ability to

_____

even when I'm tired and cranky.

20

You make me feel so

_____

whenever we're in public.

21

You are the

_____

to my

_____

22

You put up with

_____

even though I know it annoys you.

23

The way you pretend to

_____

whenever I

_____

24

I love the way we always

_____

together.

25

Your

_____

is / are the best.

26

You know exactly what to say and do to make me

_____

27

You look really hot when you

_____

28

I love that you never

_____

29

You're always willing to

_____

30

It makes me smile when you

_____

31

I love hearing your opinion on

_____

32

You're so good at

_____

33

I love how we stay up late talking about

_____

34

The way you geek out over

_____

makes me

_____

35

When you kiss me I

_____

36

The times you help me with

_____

even though I know you don't want to.

37

How you patiently explain

_____

when I don 't understand.

38

I love how you're always able to

_____

even in awkward situations.

39

The cute face you make when you're trying to

_____

40

How you always seem to know what I want when

_____

41

That we have silly fights about

_____

42

I love how I can trust you to

_____

43

The fact that you watch

_____

with me and don't complain.
(Although I think you secretly like it too)

44

The thing I admire the most about you is

_____

45

The sweet way you let me beat you at

_____

46

The way you

_____

when we watch a scary movie.

47

I love it when you share your

_____

with me.

48

You can always be relied upon to

_____

49

I love watching you when

_____

50

I love how you're not afraid to

_____

51

The way you call me your

_____

melts my heart.

52

We have the best

_____

ever.

Made in the USA
Coppell, TX
19 December 2021

69502091R00059